# ONE-MINUTE
# PRAYERS®
## for Moms

## HOPE LYDA

**HARVEST HOUSE PUBLISHERS**
EUGENE, OREGON

*Cover by Bryce Williamson*

*Cover photo © iStockphoto / Borut Trdina, pworld*

ONE-MINUTE PRAYERS is a registered trademark of The Hawkins Children's LLC. Harvest House Publishers, Inc., is the exclusive licensee of the federally registered trademark ONE-MINUTE PRAYERS.

*With gratitude and admiration for all praying moms.*

*And special thanks to my friends Anne-Renee Gumley and Amanda Bacon, the clever and caring women at* The Masterpiece Mom *blog and podcast. I appreciate and love your passion, spirit, and humor (and not just because you brought me food when I was hungry).*

**ONE-MINUTE PRAYERS® FOR MOMS**
Copyright © 2017 Hope Lyda
Published by Harvest House Publishers
Eugene, Oregon 97402
www.harvesthousepublishers.com

ISBN 978-0-7369-6664-1 (Milano Softone™)
ISBN 978-0-7369-6665-8 (eBook)
ISBN 978-0-7369-7312-0 (CBOCS)

**Printed in China**

17 18 19 20 21 22 23 24 / RDS-SK / 10 9 8 7 6 5 4 3 2 1

# Contents

# Mom, Do You Have a Minute?

How often are you beckoned by a child with the words, "Mom, come here a minute"? And after you accept the invitation, do you spend a mini-eternity fixing something that has broken into unrecognizable pieces, problem-solving a complicated homework project, or seeking out the wayward left partner of a pair of shoes that probably doesn't even fit that child anymore?

If that sounds familiar, you might hesitate to trust that a true minute is enough to do anything for yourself, let alone something that will strengthen your connection to God and to your kids. But every mom-minute matters, and the prayers in this book were created to lead you to God's presence for comfort, peace, inspiration, perspective, and hope for your life and that of your children.

Your day is full of priorities and decisions made so often on behalf of other people. May your time spent in these pages offer you nourishment and a refuge. As you pray for you and your family, you will discover the renewal that comes in the sanctuary of stillness. When you are weary, unsure, or badly in need of an adult time-out, your conversation with God will restore you to being one of the living—the living who praise the Lord and can't wait to share about His faithfulness with their children.

> The living, the living—they praise you,
>     as I am doing today;
> parents tell their children
>     about your faithfulness.
>
> Isaiah 38:19

The truth is, your children are not the only ones asking for a minute of your time. Your Creator is speaking this question to your heart. Maybe He is even shouting or whistling to get your attention over the din, dedication, and drama that fill up a mama's life. When His voice reaches your spirit, He asks if you have a moment to be in His presence right now. Go to Him. Your heart craves to be held by the One who made it. Your mind seeks wisdom and clarity. Your body needs the restoration that prayer sparks in your every cell. And your spirit's desire is to be a prayerful woman, a prayerful mom.

Let God be the one to heal the places in your life that are broken beyond recognition. Allow your Provider the time to problem-solve your family's needs by giving you a lens of discernment, faith, and truth. And step into grace so you can surrender those wayward pieces of you that are lost beneath guilt, fear, or fatigue—or that don't fit God's purpose for you anymore.

This is a minute that will lead to a full eternity of being seen and loved by your God.

Say yes.

Trust

# A Child's Faith

*Then Jesus told him, "Because you have seen
me, you have believed; blessed are those who
have not seen and yet have believed."*
JOHN 20:29

With great joy I have watched my children embrace faith. They form a sweet, innocent bond with You, and they have a second-nature awe and admiration for their Maker. I have compared this faith to my own, but the truth is, there's a big difference. I have hindsight. I have proof after proof of Your faithfulness in my life. My children don't have that history. So when I see little hands fold, little eyes close, and little lips form words of trusting prayer, I am deeply moved. I know I am witnessing those who are blessed because they are believing without seeing. They are trusting without a personal list of evidences of Your faithfulness.

It's a gift. Every day, this parenting thing…it is a gift. Thank You, Lord, for allowing me the opportunity to witness the purity of belief through the faith of my children.

# Life Is More

*Then Jesus said to his disciples: "Therefore I tell you,
do not worry about your life, what you will eat;
or about your body, what you will wear. For life is
more than food, and the body more than clothes."*

LUKE 12:22-23

In an effort to get organized and feel on top of things, I've become a master at reducing life into compartments and categories. For about five minutes, I actually fool myself into believing this ploy will keep worries at a distance. I'm a woman of faith, and yet I've resorted to these mental tricks and games. Sigh.

Lord, I am like the disciples, who were a wee bit slow to embrace the fullness of Your provision and even slower to place their trust in You. Life is more than food, bills, work schedules, report cards, carpools, bedtime battles, grocery lists, diets, and 401k plans. Life is You. Life is faith. Life is love. Life is grace. Life is trusting in You, my sweet Savior.

# All In

*Trust in the LORD with all your heart and*
*lean not on your own understanding;*
*in all your ways submit to him, and*
*he will make your paths straight.*
PROVERBS 3:5-6

I want You to be Lord in my children's lives, yet I have tried to hold on to them with every bit of my mother's heart. You've spoken to me with gentle words and asked me to release each child to Your care and purpose. And then You have watched me stubbornly grip circumstances and people until my spiritual muscles shake with exhaustion.

Now I am ready to shed the dread and fully trust You. I'm on my knees and I'm lifting up all of my life, including those I hold most dear. Yes, Lord, You will get an ear full of prayers from me in the days ahead (okay, years) because this complete surrender is new. But I'm in…all in.

## One Good Thing

*Accept one another, then, just as Christ accepted*
*you, in order to bring praise to God...May*
*the God of hope fill you with all joy and peace*
*as you trust in him, so that you may overflow*
*with hope by the power of the Holy Spirit.*
ROMANS 15:7,13

Jesus, Your acceptance of me is my model for love and loving. It is *the* good thing that I trust to lead me to all good things. I hold my family as precious, so I want to embrace them with the acceptance You have shown me. I never want my children to doubt my love or their value as Your children.

If I become critical as my own flaws and shortcomings take over my opinions and fears, tug on my spirit, Lord. Let me fully trust and lean into Your grace. I want my life to overflow with words and actions that build up my family members. Help me accept others, shortcomings and all, with a willing heart rather than conditions. That's the evidence of Your good, unconditional love at work.

# Direction

# The Gift of Your Way

*Start children off on the way they should go, and
even when they are old they will not turn from it.*
PROVERBS 22:6

I am grateful for finding the way—Your way—during my life. The journey hasn't all taken place along smooth, paved roads. But I'm thankful for the rough terrain of detours because I learned about Your grace through each twist and turn. Now, Lord, I have my heart turned toward You, and I can't imagine ever again wandering in a different direction.

This sense of devotion I have translates into a sense of hope for my children. As a mom, I've been able to share Your truths and absolute goodness. In the depths of my heart, I know this foundation will always be the safe place for them to stand to be near You. My children, even when older and world-weary, will be able to find a solid footing on Your Word and in Your way.

## The One at the Cross

*"For I know the plans I have for you," declares the
LORD, "plans to prosper you and not to harm you, plans
to give you hope and a future. Then you will call on
me and come and pray to me, and I will listen to
you. You will seek me and find me when you seek me
with all your heart. I will be found by you," declares
the LORD, "and will bring you back from captivity."*
JEREMIAH 29:11-14

Jesus, I can't help it. I want to always be the one to
hold my children's hands at the crosswalk. I want
to be the one to whisper which way they should go at
the crossroads. But I know You are the only one who
was there for them at the cross.

Your sacrifice is far beyond my own, Lord. As much
as I love my children, You love them even more. You
create their futures and form their plans with great purpose. You mold their dreams to fit those You have for
them. In every moment of every day, You await their
calls with compassion, and You will never turn away
from them when they seek Your leading. I can't always
be the one beside my children, but I know the One
who can. You give this mom such deep peace, Lord.

# Carry Me

*Then I said to you, "Do not be terrified; do not be afraid of them. The LORD your God, who is going before you, will fight for you, as he did for you in Egypt, before your very eyes, and in the wilderness. There you saw how the LORD your God carried you, as a father carries his son."*

DEUTERONOMY 1:29-31

Sleep is a rare thing for me these days. I crave it and have daydreams about the chance to experience luxuriously long night dreams. Sadly, as the evening quiet fills my house, my mind shouts its worries, and sleep is delayed. I'm jealous of how quickly children can go from stubbornly resisting bedtime to breathing heavily as they are carried to bed.

Even in my state of envy, though, I would never wish away these days in my child's life when worry does not interfere with healing rest. Instead, I plan to follow that lead and believe that You will go before me, fending off the anxious thoughts and fighting the real and imagined foes. Tonight, with innocent faith, I pray to fall into a deep, trusting slumber, knowing that You will carry me as a loving father carries his children when they finally surrender to peace.

# Guided and Glad

*Show me your ways, LORD, teach me your paths.*
*Guide me in your truth and teach me, for you are*
*God my Savior, and my hope is in you all day long.*
PSALM 25:4-5

If parenting has taught me anything, it's that I still have so much to learn. When I pay attention, I realize that I'm always learning about my family, myself, and You. Pre-child, I felt as though I had come into the full knowledge of adulthood and life. But now I know how ridiculous that security was because it was based on my limited strength and perspective. This former know-it-all is now glad to fall at Your feet and ask for guidance, insight, endurance, patience, and understanding.

Savior, You are my source for truth and hope. I wouldn't last a week as a mom without You to lean on and Your wisdom to draw from. When I get too secure in my limited grasp of anything, Lord, remind me of my need for You and Your ways. You see, I am even learning to appreciate the wisdom that comes with humility!

# Patience

## Waiting for the Promise

*When God made his promise to Abraham, since
there was no one greater for him to swear by, he
swore by himself, saying, "I will surely bless you and
give you many descendants." And so after waiting
patiently, Abraham received what was promised.*
HEBREWS 6:13-15

Why is the fulfillment of promises so hard to wait for? When a lot of time passes or a situation doesn't turn out as I pictured it, I begin to doubt. Did I hear Your voice? Did I truly sense Your leading to go forward in this way?

Abraham and Sarah had to wait and wait for Your promise of descendants to unfold; yet their experience created a legacy of hope for generations. God, You never forget Your people. And when You point to the future and the stars and say "I will bless you," You mean it. Your blessings are already in the works even if they don't fit my timeframe or my imagined outcome. Give me eyes to recognize the promises already fulfilled, and give me a patient heart so that my story sparks a legacy of faithfulness for my own family.

# Do I Have To?

*Consider it pure joy, my brothers and
sisters, whenever you face trials of many
kinds, because you know that the testing of your
faith produces perseverance. Let perseverance
finish its work so that you may be mature
and complete, not lacking anything.*

JAMES 1:2-4

I've been getting grief from my child lately, Lord. Anytime I give a direction, the response I receive is "Do I have to?" There's also a lot of moaning and groaning. During one of these rounds, I found myself saying, "You should be happy and grateful that you even have a room to clean!" Then it hit me. Yep. I have been the one moaning and groaning lately—to You.

You invite me to allow struggle to produce perseverance, but I fight the idea and ask, "Do I have to?" With new eyes, I see how I am missing the joy of allowing a trial to be transformed into the fruit of a deeper faith. I should be—no, I *am* happy and grateful that I have a home to clean, a family to care for, and a full life to turn over to You willingly.

# Move It!

*"Truly I tell you, if you have faith as small as
a mustard seed, you can say to this mountain,
'Move from here to there,' and it will move.
Nothing will be impossible for you."*
MATTHEW 17:20

Commanding a mountain to move sounds like anything but a demonstration of patience. Yet, Lord, I'm understanding Your ways more and more lately. I realize that practicing faith takes patience and intention. It's easy to miss those opportunities to trust You and to live out belief in the impossible. When the disciples were unable to rebuke a demon from a boy, they were impatient about their ability. But Jesus told them they needed faith, even in the amount of a mustard seed, to make the impossible happen. They didn't yet have that measure, but Jesus did.

I want the kind of faith that calls the remarkable into being. It might take time and patience, but I am willing, Lord. I want to move mountains in Your precious name.

# Losing Patience and Pride

*Be completely humble and gentle; be
patient, bearing with one another in
love. Make every effort to keep the unity
of the Spirit through the bond of peace.*
EPHESIANS 4:2-3

While struggling to get my family out the door this morning, my pulse rate was rising. And so was my voice. I didn't like the sound of it, Lord. I wasn't encouraging them to start the day with peace. In the middle of my ultimatums and frenzied gestures, there was no evidence of Your love and tenderness. Honestly, I think I lose patience because I ultimately want my family organized and prepared so they reflect well on me. How did pride become my motivation?

Take the pride, Lord. I want a humble spirit. I want to be present for my family with ease and a gentleness. In those moments when I am irrationally vested in how my family looks or acts, remind me that the only glory I am meant to serve is Yours. And the only well I need to draw from to serve my family is Your unconditional, unlimited love.

Joy

## Come On In

*Be joyful in hope, patient in affliction, faithful
in prayer. Share with the Lord's people
who are in need. Practice hospitality.*
ROMANS 12:12-13

Lord, fuel in me a heart that extends and expresses Your love. Keep me from hesitating when I have an opportunity to practice hospitality by giving time, shelter, or a listening ear. I want to be a joyful servant who is gracious in the face of others' needs and generous with compassion and prayers.

God, bless this home with more guests, friends, strangers, and members of my children's circle of friends, including kids on the periphery who need a welcoming space. In Your power, I can create a home where children feel safe and visitors feel wanted. I welcomed You into my heart a long time ago. Now You're calling me to welcome others into my home and heart with joy.

# Is Anyone Happy?

*Is anyone among you in trouble? Let them pray.*
*Is anyone happy? Let them sing songs of praise.*
JAMES 5:13

I caught myself faking happiness this week. Do I really believe that my friends or kids will be disappointed in me if I am more deflated than elated? God, when I'm in trouble, I follow the prescription in James 5:13 and I pray. But I've been skipping the chance to celebrate the joy of Your presence in my moments of need.

I might not be happy-go-lucky right now, but I am happy as Your child. I know You are with me in my troubles. The peace and relief of that truth makes me want to lift my voice in praise. Even when I face the darker days, Your joy resides in me, and that's something to sing about! (No faking required.)

# Learning Secrets

*I know what it is to be in need, and I know what it*
*is to have plenty. I have learned the secret of being*
*content in any and every situation, whether well*
*fed or hungry, whether living in plenty or in want.*
*I can do all this through him who gives me strength.*
PHILIPPIANS 4:12-13

Lord, I've been through some times of great need, and You have been there with me and for me. I've journeyed through emotional, physical, and fiscal struggle and come out the other side with a deep understanding of Your grace and strength. I'm in awe of how my initial fears transformed into contentment when I leaned into Your sure presence.

Having hindsight of Your power at work has given me a new frame of reference for every situation I face. When my child is anxious about a challenge or my husband is concerned about the future, I offer support and prayer from a place of peace. I'm truly getting what it means to live in Your hand and by Your hand. Thank You, Lord, for the gift of contentment.

# Pure Joy

❧

*Create in me a pure heart, O God, and renew*
*a steadfast spirit within me. Do not cast me*
*from your presence or take your Holy Spirit*
*from me. Restore to me the joy of your salvation*
*and grant me a willing spirit, to sustain me.*
PSALM 51:10-12

I haven't shouted with joy in a long, long time. An authentic, from-the-gut laugh hasn't highlighted my day since I don't know when.

Break down those barriers, Lord, between me and the absolute joy of my salvation. Let me show my children what it means to be delighted in and by You. I want to play in Your peace. I want to sing with the joy of the Holy Spirit. I want to leap with the freedom of purity and purpose. When I resist joining in on the simple silliness of children, nudge me to get over myself. Wasn't life so much better when I saw the good in everything and everyone? Restore to me the wonder of being Your child so that my life is cast in the light of Your hope.

Quiet

# In the Quiet

*The quiet words of the wise are more to be heeded than the shouts of a ruler of fools.*
ECCLESIASTES 9:17

When the world was conceived, the rush of creation, the rush of quiet, the rush of perfection must have been awesome. Lord, take me to that moment in time. Replace images of humankind's version of success with visions of Your power. Help me see what You want me to see in my life.

When my children's voices fill my every waking moment, I forget what a blessing they are. I let my attention glide over the surface of their chatter, and I miss the words You speak to me through them. Encourage my spirit to seek quiet, to reenergize, and to become healthy and aware. This I owe to my children, but also I owe it to Your child.

# Trading Busyness for Peace

*Make it your ambition to lead a quiet life.*
1 THESSALONIANS 4:11

Grant me a moment of quiet today, Lord. Maybe I will find it in unexpected places. It might be a time when I'd rather be busy or stay distracted. But coax me into Your peace. Direct my mind to thoughts of You, my family, those who need prayer.

Calm my anxieties about the risk of slowing down, doing nothing. I will step into the quiet and feel the relief from busyness. I will mentally put down the lists of tasks to perform, the chores to finish, the places to be, the plans to make. When life feels like it is spiraling downward and there is no way to stand still, bring my breath to a new depth and prepare my heart to be present to Your own. I wouldn't trade spending this moment, this space, with You for anything.

# Come with Me

*Then, because so many people were coming and*
*going that they did not even have a chance*
*to eat, he said to them, "Come with me by*
*yourselves to a quiet place and get some rest."*
MARK 6:31

From the moment I wake up until my last good nights, there is noise to fill my head and spirit. I hear requests. Demands. Instructions. Pleas. And that is on top of my own thought life. Lord, call me away from all this. My heart desires to be with You. Lead me to Your presence.

Lord, You call me by name. You prepare a place of quiet and restoration. When I enter this time of prayer You are waiting to embrace me, hold me up, and offer me strength for my journey. I have such hunger, Lord. And You offer nourishment and a place to rest my weary soul. I pray that I become this kind of refuge for my children. May I always show the way to Your quiet place.

# Rest Before Sleep

*This is what the LORD says to me: "I will remain quiet and will look on from my dwelling place, like shimmering heat in the sunshine, like a cloud of dew in the heat of harvest."*

ISAIAH 18:4

Now I lay me down to sleep…

Lord, each night I check on my children before I lie down for sleep. Following their bedtime battle, they are peaceful; their breathing is full and trusting. This sight calms me. My tight shoulders and the knots from worried thoughts loosen. I feel free to reflect on the day You have given me and to wonder about what You have for me tomorrow.

In this sweet time of rest, I can release my hold on those things I cannot control. I regret any resistance I had today to Your will. I know peace comes to those living in Your way. In the wake of my battle for control, my breathing, too, is full and trusting. Thank You, Lord.

# Transformation

# Change of Heart

*Change your laughter to mourning and*
*your joy to gloom. Humble yourselves*
*before the Lord, and he will lift you up.*
JAMES 4:9-10

Lord, experiencing the intense joy of having children has also opened up life to the possibility of great loss. I encourage my children to step out, to try new things, but all the while my heart is racing, evaluating the risk of physical or emotional hurts. Just by looking at my children's jam-covered mouths, my heart expands with pure happiness. When I watch them anguish over friendship trouble or a difficult task, though, I experience an actual physical ache.

I believe this depth of feeling is a gift from You. Never has my heart been so open, so vulnerable, and so full. I understand now how You must feel watching all Your children as they struggle, learn to love, and grow in Your will. When I imagine the sorrow of ever losing my family, Lord, call me to cherish the immense joy of today. Thank You for changing my life to encompass such passion.

# A Different Outlook

*He called a little child to him, and placed the*
*child among them. And he said: "Truly I tell you,*
*unless you change and become like little children,*
*you will never enter the kingdom of heaven."*
MATTHEW 18:2-3

God, motherhood has taught me so much. You must laugh while watching how my once perfectly scheduled, finely orchestrated life has been thrown off-kilter. Sometimes I beg to return to those days. I remember being a punctual person. I recall leaving the house confident that I did not have oatmeal on my sleeve. There was a time when I cruised the grocery store aisles without having to keep track of how many extra treats were thrown into my cart by little hands.

Just when I miss my past freedoms, You remind me to become more like children. I hear this, Lord. And I pay attention to daily minutia as well as to matters of great importance, because all of it creates this wonderful life You've given me. I am no longer preoccupied with the law of social perfection, and even when I have chocolate on my face, You first see the clean, innocent heart inside of me.

# Renewed by Your Power

*"Praise be to the name of God for ever and ever;*
*wisdom and power are his.*
*He changes times and seasons;*
*he deposes kings and raises up others.*
*He gives wisdom to the wise*
*and knowledge to the discerning."*
DANIEL 2:20-21

God, I need a miracle today. Just one. An itty-bitty change of heart. That is all. But I know it will take Your mighty hand to fill me with grace. An okay morning took a sharp turn during a breakfast serving of bickering among the children, and I need grace enough for the busy day ahead of me.

Lord, please change my heart. Impress upon my mind the affection You hold for Your children. I want to carry this with me as my model for the day. You see the shadows that fall upon my spirit when days go bad. Help me watch for the blessings that exist between the inconveniences or irritations. Mold my words so that they are uplifting and encouraging. I praise You, Lord. Your love is so powerful it can change the course of a woman's heart.

# Never Wavering

*Therefore, my dear brothers and sisters, stand
firm. Let nothing move you. Always give
yourselves fully to the work of the Lord, because
you know that your labor in the Lord is not in vain.*

1 Corinthians 15:58

Change can give birth to the miraculous. I watch my children grow inside and out. They absorb information and form concepts and beliefs. They even seek You and love You. But Lord, sometimes I try to pass off my inconsistent behavior as a change of opinion or perspective. I give in to the whims of my children when I should stay true to the guidelines my husband and I have agreed on. Yet You call me to stand firm in my belief, my understanding of truth. Please help me when I hedge slightly left or right of honesty, integrity, and love.

When I take liberties with my family's house rules, my children take note. They are piecing together the image of a life under Your authority. May I not forget this. Help me show them a worthy example. Let my path be straight, my stance firm, and my gaze steady.

Gifts

# The Fruit of Your Faithfulness

*Every good and perfect gift is from above,
coming down from the Father of the heavenly lights,
who does not change like shifting shadows. He chose
to give us birth through the word of truth, that we
might be a kind of firstfruits of all he created.*
JAMES 1:17-18

You bless me, Lord, with many gifts. When my children smile, I know I have been granted the most amazing gift of all. As I look at the course my life has taken, Your hand is evident every step of the way. From the time Your word gave birth to my soul, I have lived a rich life. I regret the times when doubt breezed through a difficult circumstance. I understand now how patience reveals Your faithfulness in all things. I want my life and my children's lives to be an offering to You. May we be patient and filled with belief.

I pray today for faith in Your unchanging ways. I flit about with human fickleness, casting shadows on the path of truth You have laid out for me. I will regain my footing on the solidity of gratitude. And here I will see the gifts fall from heaven.

# A Humble Request

*If you, then, though you are evil, know
how to give good gifts to your children, how
much more will your Father in heaven
give good gifts to those who ask him!*

MATTHEW 7:11

Jesus, my children relate to gifts with varying grace. Sometimes they show little appreciation. They make requests boldly and hold out their hands, waiting for me to comply. In a moment of shyness, they lower their eyes and voices and vaguely state a need, hoping I will understand how to solve their problem, fill their void.

Lord, I know I don't approach You with great consistency. But as my heart opens wide to the needs of my children, I have a glimpse of Your desire to bestow good gifts to those who call out to You. I will try to ask in humility, never demanding, but always with an outstretched hand to receive the love You offer. Because no matter what supplication my lips might stumble over, it is Your love that fills the void in my heart.

# Answering the Call

*God's gifts and his call are irrevocable.*
ROMANS 11:29-30

Lord, I thank You for the abilities, direction, and talents You have given me. These strengths balance out my areas of weakness. They help me serve my family and those I come in contact with. Recognizing my strengths allows me to become a helpmate to my husband.

Yet I admit I sometimes view these gifts as burdens because they challenge me to walk in the way of purpose in spite of feelings of uncertainty or even fear. Forgive me when I am reluctant to develop these areas in my life. Or when I have ignored Your leading. Help me pray even when I am busy. Guide me to say yes to those activities where my gifts can serve You. I long to embrace Your call and become a vessel that overflows with Your goodness.

# Looking for a Handout

*"All these people gave their gifts out of*
*their wealth; but she out of her poverty*
*put in all she had to live on."*
LUKE 21:4

I am poor today, Lord—poor in spirit and lacking strength. I know my children see it. They look at me with expectation, hoping I will find my way through and be present to them and for them and their needs. I was doing fine and then hit a wall. The truth is, I have been running on the memory of energy and on fabricated versions like caffeine and junk food.

I am sorry it has taken me this long to come to You. Lord, I pray for Your strength right now. My lack turns to abundance when I fall to Your feet and ask for the faith, grace, mercy, and hope You extend to me. Let the gifts that come out of my poverty be a blessing to my children. May these times of need become a testimony of Your power. When You fill my spirit and You replenish my will and desire, I am wealthy. From this restored wealth, I pray to give freely to my children, to others, and back to You, dear Lord.

# Renewal

# Secure in Your Arms

*"Let the beloved of the Lord rest secure in him,*
*for he shields him all day long, and the one*
*the Lord loves rests between his shoulders."*
DEUTERONOMY 33:12

Hold me, Lord. Oh, how I need to rest. My days have been so scattered. I call some of them productive, and some just acting out the daily grind, but all leave me weary and longing for comfort. As I wipe the forehead of a feverish kid or I bend down close to whisper good night into my child's ear, I sense Your healing touch and soothing words. I know Your tender love is always upon me.

Lead me to quiet times of meditation and calm. My body is so tired that I must lean on You throughout the day. And You are always there. Thank You, Lord, for picking up this child, cradling my heart, and offering rest for my soul.

# Looking to You

*The LORD replied, "My Presence will go
with you, and I will give you rest."*
EXODUS 33:14

I am a bit afraid of the road ahead. I see a curve, some distant signs, and a shady outline of things to come. The hazy future can keep me up at night and take over my thoughts during the day. My family and I need security, not more uncertainty. This fear of the unknown draws energy from me. I've been short with people I love, Lord. I've let my thoughts tumble toward worst-case scenarios rather than prayers of trust.

Direct my eyes to Yours so I do not lose sight of my future. Remove my fear with the promise of eternity. Do not let me forget, during this stretch of days without definition, that You are with me. My soul will be rested as I and my spirit are renewed, as I look to You and clearly see the way to go.

# Mercy Wrapped in Truth

*This is how we know that we belong to the truth,*
*and how we set our hearts at rest in his presence:*
*If our hearts condemn us, we know that God is greater*
*than our hearts, and he knows everything.*
1 John 3:19-20

God, guilt covers me like a thick, woolen blanket in the heat of summer. It scratches my skin. It makes me thirsty. I promise anything to have it removed so I can breathe. But it is Your promise, Your truth, that peels away the layers of my guilt and shame.

You are greater than my heart, with its debilitating perception of burden. You free me and give me room to breathe. The coolness of Your mercy quenches my spirit's thirst, and I am able to rest in Your grace. I belong to You, and this truth refreshes me. It changes every part of my being. Oh, Lord, how I want my children to belong to You and to know what it feels like to be released from guilt and wrapped in grace.

# Returning to Sabbath

*For six days work is to be done, but the seventh day
is a day of sabbath rest, holy to the L*ORD*.*
EXODUS 31:15

have forgotten how to rest, Lord. I bought into a non-stop lifestyle, and I'm tired of it. Lord, remove my notions that only a rigid, busy day is a productive one. Help me be fruitful without sacrificing moments of prayer, meditation, and laughter just because they are not on the schedule. My children are exposed to even more distractions than I am. I want them to experience the joy of breathing space during a day. I want them to know the restoration and happiness that can come during the quiet moments.

I won't delete my calendar—it provides security and order for me. But I will become a steward of my time so the gift of Sabbath returns to my lifestyle. Lord, open up my life to the treasure of rest. You speak to us when we are quiet. I commit to meeting You in stillness this week. It is a start.

Growth

# Growing in Hope

*Even youths grow tired and weary, and young
men stumble and fall; but those who hope
in the LORD will renew their strength.*
ISAIAH 40:30-31

God, I hear myself warn my children about their limits all the time. "You'll get tired if you carry those toys to the playground." "Your feet will blister if you wear those new shoes without socks." "Staying up too late will make tomorrow unbearable." The impact of my advice and input is minimal if my children choose not to pay attention. Recently, when I was espousing wisdom without gaining any headway, I paused and wondered how often You feel as though Your truth falls on my deaf ears. How many times have You provided me with the hopeful instruction I need but I've chosen instead to carry too much, move forward without discernment, or push my limits.

Lord, I want to listen to Your leading and proceed into situations buoyed by faith. Here I am right now, awaiting Your instruction for my day. I've grown tired of being tired. I am so ready to grow in wisdom, obedience, and hope.

# Flowering in Beauty

*I made you thrive like a plant in the field; and
you grew, matured, and became very beautiful.*
EZEKIEL 16:7 NKJV

They grow like weeds! My relatives say this about my children and it makes me laugh. How true, Lord. Their lengthening limbs tangle and intertwine at awkward stages. They blossom with colorful ideas and radiant thoughts. And they flower into new creations. God, I am in awe of watching them grow into the people You have formed them to become. I might not be wearing overalls, but my job is that of a farmer who tends to the plot of life in her charge. I need Your help to know how to nurture these sweet, growing souls I call my children! Show me what they need to rise up as creations who adore their Creator.

All living things are under Your care and sprout beneath Your watchful eye. I find such comfort in knowing that You are my children's ultimate caregiver. May their growth bring honor to You as their beauty gives the world even more proof of Your faithfulness.

# Embrace the Grace

*Grow in the grace and knowledge of our Lord and Savior Jesus Christ. To him be glory both now and forever!*

2 PETER 3:18

My children bring home homework that is more interesting and more advanced every year. I want to tell them life presents even tougher lessons. I hear them speak of dreams and goals with excitement. My first thoughts cloud with warnings of unexpected changes, forgotten dreams, or disappointment. Lord, I don't want to think of these negative outcomes and cast shadows on the bright dreams of my children. After all, I hold great hope for their future.

As Your child, I know the mysteries of life are awesome and wonderful. Don't let me forget about the amazing things You have done in my past. I want to face the unfolding future with joyful anticipation. Return to me a hunger and passion. I want my first thoughts to be of possibility in Your strength. Help me walk alongside my children as we learn and grow in Your grace together.

# Harvest Time

*"The seed will grow well, the vine will yield its fruit, the ground will produce its crops, and the heavens will drop their dew. I will give all these things as an inheritance to the remnant of this people."*

ZECHARIAH 8:12

My growth follows the order of Your creation. You craft every seed and vine; You form the shape of my heart and soul. And You know the fruit my life will bear in the future. I may act as though I know what I'm doing and where I'm going, but You are aware of my insecurities. And the list gets long! Give me guidance in all areas.

Don't let me become too comfortable in my present state of being. I want to sip of heaven's dew and be nourished by Your favor. I pray for a wise spirit that leads me to new challenges and opportunities for growth. When I feel Your nudge to step up, step out, or step onto a new path, help me trust You and follow through. I want to expand my life. I don't want to wither and fade away. My growing faith will become the inheritance of encouragement my children need for their own challenges and opportunities.

# Motherhood

# My Heavenly Parent

*"As a mother comforts her child, so
will I comfort you."*
ISAIAH 66:13

Lord, You teach me the ways of motherhood. Your gentle touch comforts me. Your precepts direct me. And Your commands keep my steps firmly on the path You make for me. But some days I feel as though I'm either faking motherhood or I have started a round of "playing house" that will not end.

On days like today, when I don't know if I can pretend one more minute, You give me a gift. A child calls out seeking my love. I mend a broken heart and fix a broken bike. And You remind me that my version of motherhood is real. And although I am not perfect, may my motherhood reflect the love of my heavenly parent.

## It's About Respect

*"Honor your father and your mother, as the LORD your God has commanded you, so that you may live long and that it may go well with you in the land the LORD your God is giving you."*

DEUTERONOMY 5:16

Jesus, mold me into a mother worthy of honor. I cannot force my children to respect me, but I can live a life that is fruitful, deeply rooted in Your truth, and overflowing with Your love. I vow to bring my children up in a godly way. I want my actions and words toward their father and my parents and in-laws to be honorable and generous so that my kids witness Your commands obeyed with gladness and gratitude.

How wonderful that You desire life to go well for me and for my children—for all Your children. You are a merciful, kind, and giving God worthy of respect and admiration. I will remind my children of this every day as I encourage them to walk toward the promised land You prepare for them. It is my great honor to do so.

# Correct Me If I'm Wrong

*"Teach me, and I will be quiet; show
me where I have been wrong."*
JOB 6:24

Correct me, Lord. When You see me acting out or acting up, correct my ways. When I discipline my children, I fear they don't sense the love behind my stern voice or pointed finger. But the love is there, and it is so deep. I think of this when I hear Your words of correction or You guide my steps with the force of an unexpected happening. Help me sense Your deep love for me during these times.

Motherhood is all about the practice and discipline of love. Thank You for being my example, Lord. You want only the best for me. I want only the best for my children. Teach me, and show me where I have been wrong. Give me a heart sensitive to instruction so I can turn toward all that is right in Your eyes.

# Becoming Me

*Our people must learn to devote themselves
to doing what is good, in order to provide for
urgent needs and not live unproductive lives.*
TITUS 3:14

God, as a child, I had many visions of what I might become. "What do you want to be when you grow up?" was a question I welcomed. My answer changed nearly every time. I prayed for You to bless my choice of the day. Now that I am a mother, I understand what it is to be committed to a vision, a purpose. You have given me this clarity.

I have other responsibilities and hold other positions, but motherhood is an act of devotion. I care for my family and provide for their needs. I build them up with truths from Your Word. When it is dark, I point to Your light. And when my children dream of becoming something special, I pray You will bless their choice of the day.

Life

# The Good Life

*Surely your goodness and love will follow
me all the days of my life, and I will
dwell in the house of the Lord forever.*

PSALM 23:6

La Dolce Vita, the sweet life. This is the Christian life. My existence is based upon a foundation of Your grace and goodness. Lord, help me taste the sweetness of my days. To sip from a cup of divine nectar. Help me instill in my kids a sense of wonder as we delight together in Your goodness. When my attitude or immediate circumstances turn sour, let me wave unpleasantries and annoyances aside and embrace the flavorful, abundant life. I want my children to get excited about life's treasures when I point out the deep blue of the sea, the shimmer of the rain-kissed leaves, and the tender graces we witness as a family day in and day out.

Thank You for filling my heart with hope's promise. I am fortunate, happy, and joyful because I reside in Your house forever.

# The Ups and Downs

*Guard my life and rescue me; do not let me
be put to shame, for I take refuge in you.*
PSALM 25:20

Oh, Lord. Lord, rescue me from myself. Recently I stumbled over my arrogance. I spoke when silence was much more appropriate. I didn't hurt anyone, but I made a fool of myself and I didn't reflect Your goodness. Still, You picked me up and let me continue. But the sting of humiliation echoes long past an awkward moment of failure.

Lord, protect me from my own selfish whimsy. Calm my mind so I think first. Pray first. Consider silence or caution an option. It would be nice to not require Your refuge so often, but in the meantime, may others forget my indiscretions and recall only my redeemer.

# Life's Riches

*A person's riches may ransom their life, but the*
*poor cannot respond to threatening rebukes.*
PROVERBS 13:8

I am surrounded by elements of bondage, Lord. Material wealth, modern conveniences, advanced technology…these evidences of achievement anchor me to the earth and the world's ways. Anyone or any one misfortune could hold my life hostage by threatening the safety and future of these empty "things." Why do I place so much emphasis on the accrual and maintenance of such trappings?

Free my mind to exist as a pauper, Lord. Guide my choices so my children learn how Your priorities are the only priorities. Give me the wisdom to release false needs and replace them with elements a servant requires. As I fall to my knees, worldly prosperity falls away. But I am not threatened by possible destruction or destitution. My wealth flows from a limitless source: grace.

# A Covenant to Create

*I will remember my covenant between me and you
and all living creatures of every kind. Never again
will the waters become a flood to destroy all life.*
GENESIS 9:15

Lord, I hold Your promises so close to my heart. When the world fails me, I have faith in Your love. When I perceive the flood waters rising, let me stand confident on the foundation of Your covenant. I pray for my children to have unwavering assurance in their relationship with You so their trials become invitations to trust You even more.

Out my kitchen window I see evidence of Your commitment to create and not to destroy. I am thankful for nature's beauty. The aesthetics and intricacies are wondrous. But it is the abundance and preservation of Your creation that remind me how much You love life.

Longing

# Sigh of the Times

*All my longings lie open before you, LORD;*
*my sighing is not hidden from you.*
PSALM 38:9

Lately I have been sighing a lot. Too much. I'm sure You've heard me, Lord. And I'm sure You know how much I frown upon this generic expression of disappointment when my children force their breath at the dinner table, heave their chests when ground rules have been set, and roll their eyes for emphasis when I reprimand their behavior. Yet in my prayers to You, I have been sighing. At first it is just an expression of fatigue. But over time it becomes a phrase of discontentment. This attitude says, *You have failed me, Lord. You don't understand me. You have not met my deepest needs.*

Forgive me, Lord, for this embarrassing self-indulgence. Erase my disappointment and take hold of my life. Shift my perspective toward gratitude and faith. Embed righteous longings deep within my soul so my sighs are replaced by songs and praises.

# Serving the Needs of the Lord

*Those who were sent ahead went and found it
just as he had told them. As they were untying the
colt, its owners asked them, "Why are you untying
the colt?" They replied, "The Lord needs it."*
LUKE 19:32-34

What do you need, Lord?" This is not a question I ask very often, or even think to pray about. I focus on my needs whenever a listening ear is made available. I know You are all-mighty, all-powerful, and therefore do not require my assistance to accomplish anything. But just the same…What can I do for You today, Lord?

Have You been asking for an extra hand recently? Is there some simple or significant need You want me to fill as Your servant and disciple? A family across town needs help to make ends meet. My husband longs for me to really hear his hopes and dreams. One of my children's friends craves encouragement. Are You watching and longing for me to step into a life of assurance and faith? I am here, Lord. Please guide me and use me to fulfill Your plan.

# More Than Lip Service

*If one of you says to them, "Go in peace; keep warm
and well fed," but does nothing about their physical
needs, what good is it? In the same way, faith by
itself, if it is not accompanied by action, is dead.*
JAMES 2:16-17

Jesus, I gave someone the brush-off recently and I
feel bad. Forgive me for dismissing a genuine and
deep need because I was in a hurry. Remind me of the
blessings in my life, all of which are from You. Remind
me I do not make it through any day without the kindness of others. Remind me of grace. Stop me before I
speak those simple phrases that rise in my throat, such as:

"I'm sure things will be looking up in no time."

"If that becomes a big problem, let me know."

"God will work it out."

Turn my platitudes into "How can I serve you?"—
an expression of Your active grace. Inspire me to reach
out to my children in the same way. Let my questions
and my times of listening and helping be authentic and
always from the heart.

# Getting Over Myself

*The Lord will guide you always; he will
satisfy your needs in a sun-scorched land
and will strengthen your frame.*
ISAIAH 58:11

Lord, my daily prayers seem to revolve around my needs. I am blinded by them. I can go for days and just wallow in them. Do you tire of my selfish rants? I do. I fill our quiet moments with a long list of requirements. I feel like I give to others so much during my day. They are people I love, but the act of giving takes so much. By the time I fall before You, I am bursting with my needs, my wants, my longings in life.

I am right to go to You, Lord, to fill my needs. But give me a heart for the needs of others. Show me the hurts of my children so I can ease their burdens with the balm of faith. Lead me to a place of praise and worship so I can express my love for You. And help me see how much I am receiving in those times of giving.

Worry

# When Hearts Talk

*Do not worry about tomorrow, for tomorrow will worry about itself. Each day has enough trouble of its own.*
MATTHEW 6:34

I like to listen to my children's nighttime prayers. When I hear their voices lifted up to You, I am gaining a glimpse of their hearts, their concerns, and their worries. I understand what preoccupies those active minds through words that surface as soon as they fold their hands and bow their heads. I see the relief and release cross their faces when they say "Amen."

Is this what happens when I pray? Do You see a vulnerable heart willing to share its fears? Or have I forgotten how to really talk to You? Lord, strip me of my clichéd petitions and prayers of thanksgiving. Let me bow down and tell You about my worries and express my list of praises; I have many of both. Let me give my life over to You like a trusting child.

# Ready or Not

*Make up your mind not to worry beforehand
how you will defend yourselves. For I will
give you words and wisdom that none of your
adversaries will be able to resist or contradict.*

LUKE 21:14-15

Jesus, I cannot help it. I get defensive. I'm a worrier. You have heard my prayers throughout the day and know how much I stew over what will happen next, what someone will say, what my response will be. It is exhausting. I pray for peace during these times. I pray to trust You implicitly with each and every situation I face.

Guide me to be filled with Your Word and Your wisdom. Let it fall from my lips at the right moment. May I never take my faith in You and twist it into arrogance. Allow me the peace that is born of trust. Today, Lord, I will not waste one minute fretting. This is the day the Lord has made, and I will rejoice in it!

## In Your Time

*Humble yourselves, therefore, under God's mighty hand, that he may lift you up in due time. Cast all your anxiety on him because he cares for you.*
1 PETER 5:6-7

God, I come to You today with silly frustrations. I asked my husband to take care of something weeks ago, Lord, and it remains undone. Now I am obsessed with this lingering task. If it isn't one thing, it's another. I distort the importance of a simple problem, when the real situation that needs fixing is ignored. I hold on to the wrong things and then let the precious threads of life and love slip away.

Lord, You know how my heart needs to be healed. You know each relationship that is strained or torn. Release me from anxiety and anger. I bow down, beneath Your hand, and pray for You to fix my brokenness in Your time. Right now I cast my anxieties on You because You can handle them and clearly I can't. I pray I will be in Your presence and following Your way when You are ready to lift me up.

# Joy After the Storm

*When anxiety was great within me, your consolation brought joy to my soul.*
PSALM 94:19

When waves of worry crash down on me, I look for refuge in Your arms. Your embrace is strong and certain and You lift me high above the roar of concern. The safety of Your firm grip allows me to release my fears into the air. The storm that threatened my life, my sanity, my happiness is now transformed. In the mist I see the colors of the rainbow and my anxiety turns to joy. You are amazing, Lord. You bring radiance to a darkened soul. I hope I learn from this intimate encounter with Your grace. When my children face these same storms, I pray that my actions and words always point upward. You console every heart. Grant us ease and peace, Lord.

Future

# Hope for Today and Tomorrow

*There is surely a future hope for you,*
*and your hope will not be cut off.*
PROVERBS 23:18

Lord, when the day feels dark, there is a future hope in You. When I am unsure about the outcome of a circumstance, You offer hope. When I pray for my children's future, there is hope. Your gift of certain assurance and hope surrounds me and covers me. I have discovered that the hard times ground me deeper in Your promises. If there is a struggle, I spend more time examining Your promises and holding them up to the light, where they cast rainbows across anything I face. In these times my faith is formed, defined, and strengthened.

In my children's lives, there is some uncertainty brewing. Give me the words to say that will encourage belief in Your presence and absolute faith in Your hope for this very moment and the days ahead. There is such peace in this sweet truth.

# Building on a Right Spirit

*Your beginnings will seem humble,*
*so prosperous will your future be.*
JOB 8:7

God, mine is a simple life. Extremely busy, yes. But still, my authentic needs are straightforward. I want my family to be healthy, loving, and walking in Your way. Personally, I want to be productive, useful, and kind. Humble my spirit, dear God, and purify my heart. Empty me of selfish ambition. Fill me with an enduring spirit.

Strengthen my wisdom so that I build up my children in righteousness and encourage their growth step by step. I pray today for the treasures of their future. May their abundance in life be found in a godly spouse, a faith-filled community, a purpose, a conviction to serve You, and a knowledge that all they have comes from Your unlimited grace. These are the simple and essential pieces to a good and righteous life. I realize that my future is prosperous if my children grow up rich in faith!

# My Child's Future

*Consider the blameless, observe the upright;*
*a future awaits those who seek peace.*
PSALM 37:37

Lord, help me raise peace-filled children who will become peace-loving adults. It's not easy to filter the world's violence and tendency toward insensitive self-preservation. When examples of evil enter our lives, let us pray over them. Teach me to teach my children a godly approach to worldly problems. I don't ever want apathy to be our response to the hurts of others and the needs of people far and near. If envy and a spirit of retaliation rise up in us, convict us, Lord, so that our hearts soften and our perspective shifts toward the perspective You reveal.

I pray for my children and the future they will walk through. May their hope always be placed in You so their responses to people and circumstances, even those that are overwhelming or scary, are made from love and not fear. The future is so much brighter when it is illuminated by Your grace.

## The Gift for Generations

*Let this be written for a future generation, that a
people not yet created may praise the LORD: "The
LORD looked down from his sanctuary on high, from
heaven he viewed the earth, to hear the groans of
the prisoners and release those condemned to death."*
PSALM 102:18-20

Mired in the details of today, I can forget what a gift
the future is for me and my family. Generations
will follow in our steps. Lord, I pray for future members
of my lineage who will serve You and carry faith into
the future. You will offer them the same grace You offer
us now. Your gift does not change. May there always
be ears to hear the message of Your salvation and may
there always be hearts to receive its hope. How can I
plant seeds today that will make an impact on the next
generations? It's a great responsibility to invest in the
freedom and faith of Your future children.

I take comfort in knowing my children will always
have You in their lives. They might stray, question, or
have doubts, but You will not leave them. My children's
children will have a chance to know You and to live for
You. In the present I pray with thanksgiving for the
grace You will extend in the future.

# The Home Front

# The Discipline of Discipline

*Whoever heeds life-giving correction*
*will be at home among the wise.*
PROVERBS 15:31

I want my children to be counted among the wise as they grow older. Lord, help me ground them in Your truths as they face life's twists and turns. It's easy to become weary when it's time to discipline or instruct my kids. But if I want them to seek Your face in all circumstances, then now and then I need to be strong and faithful in my role as the deliverer of life-giving correction! I pray for strength for my husband and me as we discipline our children with godly instruction that comes from Your way, Your Word.

Let my children make their way in the world by making their home in Your kingdom. Infuse them with Your wisdom so they are armed with Your power each day of their lives...even those days that stretch beyond my lifetime. I want them to lean into Your strength with the same certainty they would have if they leaned into an oak tree or on the shoulder of their father. Thank You for hearing the pleas of a mother. My security is in You.

# Staying True

*I will conduct the affairs of my house with*
*a blameless heart. I will not look with*
*approval on anything that is vile.*
PSALM 101:2-3

Practice what you preach. This is an easy directive to espouse, but I catch myself wandering from its truth. God, I want to be consistent in character, yet I find myself speaking a white lie when I think it saves time or preserves someone's pride—including my own. Or I put aside the obvious needs of another because I have tunnel vision directed on my tasks at hand. When I am away from the watchful eyes of my family, I am even more likely to settle for behavior that doesn't glorify You.

Lord, I pray to be an example in the way I live my life at home and when I am away. Let me enter my house with a blameless, pure heart. I do not want a double standard to crack the foundation I am building for my family. I thank You for the accountability I feel to my family and Your truth.

# Finding My Way Home

*Even the sparrow has found a home,*
*and the swallow a nest for herself,*
*where she may have her young—*
*a place near your altar,*
*Lord Almighty, my King and my God.*
PSALM 84:3

As a child, I witnessed many different definitions of home. Some were not models of godliness or love, Lord. You know I entered into family life with a bit of hesitation. In my excitement to move into a future, I had moments of fear. How young I was in my faith then. I thought I was building a home on my own. Now I understand how You preserved me and continue to preserve me. You lift me up when I struggle, and You protect my nest and my young as I find my footing in Your wisdom.

My home is near the altar of Your heart. Guide everything I do or say within the circle of my family. I want us to draw near to You, and I want our hearts to become a home for You.

# Open Heart, Open Home

*They can urge the younger women
to love their husbands and children,
to be self-controlled and pure, to be busy at home,
to be kind, and to be subject to their husbands,
so that no one will malign the word of God.*
TITUS 2:4-5

Lord, I can be intimidated by the younger generation. I could let this weakness continue, but it keeps me from opening up my home and my heart to those who need to hear about You. As my children grow older, may I seek ways to connect with them and their friends. I pray You will direct me toward mentor relationships with young women and supportive friendships with other moms.

I want to model Your love. Help me be humble about my imperfections. My past mistakes strengthen my testimony of Your grace. Even though the prospect is a little scary, I pray today to step beyond my comfort zone with the intention to share You, demonstrate Your strength, and glorify Your name.

# Protection

# Walking Under Your Protection

*But let all who take refuge in you be glad;*
*let them ever sing for joy.*
*Spread your protection over them,*
*that those who love your name may rejoice in you.*
PSALM 5:11

I rejoice in You, Lord. I celebrate my faith today. My clouds of sorrow have cleared and I see the clear sky of Your face. I cannot hold back my song of thanksgiving. My usual anxiety and frustration are replaced by peace. I am walking under Your protection because I know and love Your name.

Forgive me for the many days I avoided Your refuge. My lips trembled with fear, yet I refused to move forward. I acted like a child resisting a mother's safe embrace. Now I run to You and the security You offer. The clouds might return, but my fear will not.

# A Secure Shelter

*You are my hiding place;*
*you will protect me from trouble*
*and surround me with songs of deliverance.*
PSALM 32:7

Life and love make us vulnerable, Lord. The world's skyscrapers, mountains, and canyons cannot enclose an exposed soul. There is only one resting place for our spirits, and that is within Your encircled arms. I pray for Your hand to maneuver me and my children through trouble. Push us through the cry of defeat and into the song of deliverance. Let us stand firm in truth and faith as a family united. Do not let us hide from the challenges You bring our way. You are not a reason to step away from difficulty; You are *the* reason to run to the fire and show Your faithfulness. Help me discern what fires my children face currently so I can knowingly build their confidence in You.

Thank You, God, for being my hiding place in this land of faulty shelters. Let my belief and perseverance be a testimony to Your goodness.

# Watching Wisdom

*Do not forsake wisdom, and she will protect*
*you; love her, and she will watch over you.*
PROVERBS 4:6

I am attentive in the presence of wisdom, Lord—Your wisdom. Wisdom is the image of a grandmother—surprisingly strong, faithful, all-knowing—with a soft voice that fills my head like no shout ever could. I sit in audience on the porch, awaiting a lesson for the day. I watch her moves closely because the space between words is the birthplace for truth.

Lord, help me take on the character of wisdom. May my children watch me closely and see Your mannerisms, Your love, Your actions between words. When my children lose their way from home, may they be led back to the presence of wisdom. She sits on the porch and welcomes each of us to return home to Your presence.

# The Safe Way

*Discretion will protect you, and understanding will guard you.*

PROVERBS 2:11

God, discretion is so rare it has become an old-fashioned notion. We are all eager to move forward, to be cutting edge, and to be spontaneous. Nobody wants to hold back when making a decision or a judgment. Lord, guide me in the use of discretion and help me to teach my children the ways of the humble and shrewd. They are even more eager to run ahead or to speak quickly without thinking.

Let me learn and parent from my past errors in judgment. Allow my actions to be calm and honorable. I want to show my children the gift of waiting on Your leading so their first response will be to pause and turn toward You. I pray that they will wait patiently for Your voice so they can walk in understanding and under Your protection.

Wonder

# Blessed Vision

*Many, LORD my God,*
*are the wonders you have done,*
*the things you planned for us.*
*None can compare with you;*
*were I to speak and tell of your deeds,*
*they would be too many to declare.*

PSALM 40:5

Lord, the daily miracles I see so clearly are often lost on those who do not know You. I understand how privileged I am to be counted as one of Your own. I weep when I think of all the wonders I missed during my years of blindness. This is why I point out Your beauty and power to my children whenever I can. Until their hearts take hold of You with a firm grip of faith, I am their eyes, I am their witness, I am their guide.

Lord, when others shrug at my claims of the miraculous infusing my daily routine, encourage me to continue sharing what I know as truth. I have been where they stand. I know that in the edge of their peripheral vision, they see rays of Your light. My certainty shakes their doubt to its deceptive core. And they are that much closer to witnessing the wonders in their lives.

# Love Revealed

*Show me the wonders of your great love,*
*you who save by your right hand*
*those who take refuge in you from their foes.*
PSALM 17:7

When my children run to You, Lord (and I know they will one day soon), grant them the assurance You have given me. Shower Your love on them. They are at an advantage—children exist in a world of wonder. Doubt rarely steals their belief when they need it. Their connection to Your loving presence is as natural as the bond between mother and child.

Will my children always look to the sky with delight and awe? Will stars always shine forth Your light and guide them to the birthplace of salvation? Will the winds of truth lead them to refuge? Lord, hear my prayers. When I am not able to point out Your marvels, may the miracles of Your hand rise up and make themselves known.

## You Are Brilliant, Lord

*I stand in awe of your deeds, LORD. Renew*
*them in our day, in our time make them*
*known; in wrath remember mercy.*
HABAKKUK 3:2

In these times, the wonder of man's invention and
seemingly independent success takes the limelight
away from You. How easily we let go of what is true,
forgetting who is in charge of our days. We watch
the famous, rich, and powerful and think surely they
reached the pinnacle of society via their own devices.
Such thoughts put our faith at risk because they lead us
to believe we are responsible for blessings. Our wonder
is to be directed toward You, the creator of deeds and
results that inspire awe. Oh, how tempting it is sometimes to want the glory and worldly credentials.

When I witness my kids oohing and aahing over the
latest rising celebrity, I will remind them how "ordinary"
life shines and glitters when it is lived in Your purpose
for us. A light cast from a secondary source to create the
spotlight is really powerless. But the light that comes
from the true Light is life-giving, life-changing, and
illuminates the only path to fulfillment. You dazzle us,
Lord. Truly.

# Too Many to Count

*He performs wonders that cannot be fathomed, miracles that cannot be counted.*

JOB 5:9

One. Two. Three. Four. Fifty. Keeping track of Your miracles is something I can proudly say is no longer possible. There are too many to count. In my past I said, "I'm still waiting to see a miracle." That was when I was blind to Your wonders. My new vision of faith is one of the biggest miracles of all.

Lord, I am a humble servant kneeling before You. Your works are brilliant and amazing. How thankful I am to witness the mystery of Your goodness. I see Your hand in the simplest and most complex situations. I'm stunned by Your grace in times of trial. My heart leaps with exuberance in times of joy. May my prayers of gratitude be as plentiful as the miracles I see today.

# Discipline

# Showing Mercy

*Just as you who were at one time disobedient to God*
*have now received mercy as a result of their disobedience,*
*so they too have now become disobedient in order that they*
*too may now receive mercy as a result of God's mercy to you.*
*For God has bound all men over to disobedience*
*so that he may have mercy on them all.*
ROMANS 11:30-32

Our fallible ways bring us full circle to Your mercy, Lord. And my children—just like all Your children—are going to be disobedient. I pray for a softened heart toward them. I want to offer grace and mercy in Your likeness. This can be hard for me, maybe because I don't always extend grace to myself. For years I didn't think I was allowed to make mistakes. I carried a load that was unrealistic. And honestly, I still take on too much responsibility out of guilt or a false sense of control, rather than a desire to serve.

Lord, I ask You to fill me with Your mercy. Until this gift affects me, I will carry a cross of martyrdom, and I will pass along to my children a negative attitude about following Your will. Change my motive for discipline from "works" to "faith" so that I may relinquish control and receive Your mercy.

## Joy in Discipline

*Buy the truth and do not sell it—*
*wisdom, instruction and insight as well.*
*The father of a righteous child has great joy;*
*a man who fathers a wise son rejoices in him.*
Proverbs 23:23-24

When my patience is worn thin, I forget about the reserves of my Lord. It is my children who remind me to turn to You. Stuck in traffic and late for an appointment, I am thinking about the consequences of rescheduling and the domino effect of missing one item on my to-do list. But my children suggest we talk to You. There it is. Wisdom coming forth from the little people strapped into car seats.

I thank You for their pure hearts. Their immediate response is to pray, to run to You, and to seek Your guidance. Lord, I rejoice in my children and their love for You. They lead this controlling, worrying adult to the true source of life and wisdom—Your faithful presence.

# Relying on Your Power

*They disciplined us for a little while as they
thought best; but God disciplines us for our
good, in order that we may share in his holiness.*
HEBREWS 12:10

Lord, guide me in Your way. I was raised to know right from wrong. To be a good and fair person. But I still struggle with following a disciplined Christian life. I believe in the power of the cross. My spirit is not ruled by the law, but by Your power. Help me embrace Your holiness and lean not upon my understanding of the world, but Your knowledge of the way. You see what lies ahead for me and my family. I pray to trust the steps You show me. When I wake up tomorrow morning, I want my first thought to be "Let me live in Your power, Lord. Make me a holy partner in this life."

God, create in me a disciplined heart that is not easily sidetracked. This busy life is packed with distractions, few of which are worthy of my time or Your time. I pray to fully experience the good of Your path.

# Staying on the Path

*Be still before the Lord*
*and wait patiently for him;*
*do not fret when people succeed in their ways,*
*when they carry out their wicked schemes.*

Psalm 37:7

Lord, to continue with the way You have set before me takes great control. And oh does it ever require patience! Allow me to access You as my source of strength and endurance. I see new opportunities and want to head toward them rather than stay disciplined along this path. When someone I know achieves a level of success I desire or seems to live life with extra ease, my heart is covetous. Forgive me for comparing my journey to that of another. Calm my spirit so I can wait for Your leading.

I want only to be the me You created me to be. Your will takes me on a certain course. When I grow lazy in my pursuit of the prize that awaits me, please prod me forward. I don't want to be tempted by a false joy. Inspire me to stay steadfast, disciplined, and prepared to receive the blessings made just for me.

*Peace*

# The Cleansing Power of Peace

*For God is not a God of disorder but of peace.*
1 CORINTHIANS 14:33

I want everything in place, Lord. I labor compulsively to keep up with my home, family, and work…but the pieces refuse to fall into place. This failure does not deter me. Yet I know the order I try to bring out of my chaos is a tidy version of truth. A worldly sense of perfection. It does not breathe peace into my soul and home. Only You do this.

When I am frantically cleaning my home instead of playing with my children, grant me Your order of importance. When I envy a neighbor's new car and yet do not give money to the needy, bring my sense of justice in line with Your way. I long to have my choices and actions in line with Your best. This is the glory of living a life based on the values You call my heart to embrace.

# Back to the Flock

*As a shepherd looks after his scattered flock*
*when he is with them, so will I look after my sheep.*
*I will rescue them from all the places where they*
*were scattered on a day of clouds and darkness.*
EZEKIEL 34:12

I have strayed from the protected hillside. My independent streak pushes me to the furthest ridge. Undaunted, I continue to wander down a path of my choosing rather than the way You have cleared for me. But in a short time, my legs grow weak and I lose my footing. I am hungry, lost, and in danger. Now I pray Your eyes will fall upon me. How I miss the security and peaceful assurance of my Shepherd's leading. I call out to You, eager to make known my hiding places. Lord, find this stray lamb. You are faithful. Smiling, You rescue me. I cling to You as You carry me home.

I have experienced the love of the Shepherd. And I have so much peace knowing You will seek out and rescue my children from the places they might go during their lifetime. My family is under Your watchful, protective gaze. We rest here with gratitude.

# Order of Your Kingdom

*Since we are receiving a kingdom that
cannot be shaken, let us be thankful, and so
worship God acceptably with reverence and
awe, for our "God is a consuming fire."*
HEBREWS 12:28-29

Thanks to You, my life is set firmly on unshakable ground. No matter what comes my way, I stand on the rock of Your security. Fault lines spread out like fingers across the landscape of my life, but they do not stop my journey. Wind makes its boisterous way across the surrounding fields, tossing rootless life…but I do not change direction. Fires blush my cheeks with heat but do not scorch my desire to continue.

I am able to be strong for and with my family in the midst of change and seasons of risk because Your command brings order to the chaos. May my children see this and understand Your gracious power. May they be consumed by awe in You forever. Thank You, Lord, for the peace of Your enduring kingdom.

# Preparing the Way

*"In the wilderness prepare
the way for the Lord;
make straight in the desert
a highway for our God."*
ISAIAH 40:3

The wilderness of my crazy existence is hardly an ideal environment for You. Yet I am trying to forge a road through the chaos to make room for Your passing. This is not easy for me. I have grown accustomed to the mess surrounding my heart and mind. Could You free me from my ties to all this clutter? It is my love for You that insists upon this drastic change. I want Your peace to be my motivation and my catalyst for walking in a new way.

Your presence surrounds me. I turn to You for help and understanding. I must prepare a soul worthy of Your presence within. Make my thoughts pure. Transform my self-absorbed intentions into longings for the greater good. Give me a gracious spirit as a mom. And make straight the road that leads my life to Your purpose.

# Identity

# Called by Name

*Lift up your eyes and look to the heavens:*
*Who created all these?*
*He who brings out the starry host one by one*
*and calls forth each of them by name.*
ISAIAH 40:26

Lord, I try to fill a kaleidoscope of roles: Mother. Wife. Friend. Neighbor. Each title offers many new hats to wear. As I step into a role, I pray You are able to recognize *me* as the one You created. Remove any false sense of self that lies within my soul. May I walk along the path You have carved out of time just for me.

Lord, You call the stars by name, and You will call Your children home by name. Direct me according to Your design. Today, I lay claim to the most important identity of all—child of God.

# Life's Accessories

*Your beauty should not come from outward
adornment, such as elaborate hairstyles and
the wearing of gold jewelry and fine clothes.
Rather, it should be that of your inner self, the
unfading beauty of a gentle and quiet spirit,
which is of great worth in God's sight.*
1 PETER 3:3-4

Lord, help me not buy into the concept of designer lifestyles. I see how it distorts the value of people. Just when I have a sense of my worth in Your eyes, I compare my income, possessions, or opportunities with those of another. I deceive myself into thinking these are matters of importance. I want Your priorities to be mine. I want Your perspective to be mine.

Show me the beauty of my inner self—the part of me that calls out to You and receives Your presence. Silence the destructive voices that criticize my life. I don't want such deceptions to reach the hearts of my children. Help me reveal to them the beauty and worth of their spirit so that they recognize and illuminate that value in others.

## Knowing What Matters

*What good is it for someone to gain the whole*
*world, and yet lose or forfeit their very self?*
Luke 9:24-26

In this world of upgrades, "new and improved" products, and technological advancements, how do I show my children that they themselves are complete and perfect in You? They have learned to watch for the next big thing and do not understand the value of the here and now. God, may I speak words of encouragement to their hearts so they see significance in what they do today.

Lord, please give my children contentment. Let them savor gifts from You and not look beyond their current blessings. May their successes, large and small, turn their hearts to worship and praise. And may they never accept a substitute for the life of truth You grant them.

## You Know My Soul

*You know me, Lord;*
*you see me and test my thoughts about you.*
JEREMIAH 12:3

My children think I am a mind reader when I predict their actions and reactions. I am able to do this because I know them so well. You know each of Your children on an even more intimate level. You see the scars we hide. You uncover the memories we bury. And You remove the sins we try to cover.

When I come to You with my bag of requests, worries, and questions, You are already familiar with these concerns. You know my every thought before it turns to action. You see my future with all its mistakes and triumphs. My whole identity is found in the One who made me. I want to conduct myself to represent You—the Creator who knows every part of me and *still* loves me. Help me convey that unconditional love to my children, my husband, my family, and the people You bring into my days.

# Surrender

# *The Freedom of Righteousness*

*When you were slaves to sin, you were free from the control of righteousness. What benefit did you reap at that time from the things you are now ashamed of? Those things result in death! But now that you have been set free from sin and have become slaves of God, the benefit you reap leads to holiness, and the result is eternal life.*

ROMANS 6:20-22

Sin can enter a heart or a home under the guise of freedom. Lord, don't let me or my family fall for this trap. A life lived apart from righteousness doesn't produce love and faith; it creates an emptiness and sense of futility. I have experienced this place of loss, God. I know the pain of sin's control.

Lead me to Your freedom. I long for the clarity that comes with giving one's heart over to Your lead and nurturing. Only then can I see through today's wants to Your kingdom. I surrender control over my life, Lord. When I release my way, I am able to embrace Your way. Show me how to walk, love, speak, act, and parent in this path of freedom.

# Too Stubborn to Submit

*Submit to one another out of reverence for Christ.*
EPHESIANS 5:21

Sometimes I am too stubborn to give in, Lord—even when I see how it's the right thing to do. I refused to release my hold on a recent situation and now I have regrets. Forgive me if I hurt the feelings of another. Forgive me for modeling such a reluctant spirit to my children. Somehow submitting to You has been an easier concept to grasp than submitting to others. I worry about setting a bad example for my kids. I want them to know the gift of humbling oneself to serve others.

Help me, Lord. When I search my mind for all the reasons *not* to submit to another person, remind me what it means to serve in Your name. Break my spirit of control. Let me feel the weight of Your hand on my back as You direct me, to know that by trusting others, I am trusting You. Give me the desire to be vulnerable, open, and ready for each opportunity to be Your hands, heart, and love for another.

# Giving It Over

*"Submit to God and be at peace with him;*
*in this way prosperity will come to you."*
JOB 22:21

sense that I have held You back, Lord. I know You are able to do all things. I don't really think I could stop You from accomplishing anything, but I don't always partner with You like I should. I don't give You control of the deepest places in my heart. Your power commands my respect. I witness Your faithfulness in the lives of others and in my own family. Still, I face You while clenching a bag of situations, attitudes, and dreams behind my back. I think that maybe You won't notice that these pieces of my life are still in my possession. I hold tight to my children and leave little room for faith to lead. I hold fast to human measures of prosperity that are of no eternal value.

Forgive me for my stubbornness, Lord. Today I will reach into my bag of hang-ups and give You one…or two. Be patient with me.

# Letting the Spirit Take Charge

*You, however, are not in the realm of the
flesh but are in the realm of the Spirit, if
indeed the Spirit of God lives in you.*
ROMANS 8:9

My children are still new to understanding the differences between the realm of the flesh and that of the Spirit. I pray for a deepening of understanding and awareness in their young hearts. What a gift it will be for them to draw on the power of the Spirit of God within them. You will guide their ways. You will pull them back from harm. And You will infuse them with hope.

Today I pray for my kids' future willingness to put You in charge and keep You in charge of their needs, decisions, actions, and longings. When the temptation to give in to the leading of flesh is great, may their belief in Your goodness and truth be even greater. I want them to be able to recall specific examples from their life under my roof when we obediently made choices in the spirit and not in the flesh. Let each day of our life together as a family be a day that draws my children to depend on You rather than on the world.

*Youth*

# You Lead the Young

*Since my youth, God, you have taught me,
and to this day I declare your marvelous deeds.*
PSALM 71:17

My stomach seems to leap into my throat as I watch my children play on a rickety playground swing set or head down the street on their bikes with a group of friends. I have to remind myself of Your faithfulness back in my youth. You were with me so many times when I was certain I was running free and alone. When I was trying to stay out of range of the eyes on the back of my mother's head, You were right there beside me.

The fact that I am still alive is indeed Your marvelous doing. Lord, give me faith to turn my children over to You. Help me place the days of their youth in Your protective care. Even with my super-power mother vision, I know there will be days when they venture far from view, thinking they are alone, only to be guided by their heavenly Father.

# Restoring Youth

*Praise the LORD, my soul,*
*and forget not all his benefits...*
*who satisfies your desires with good things*
*so that your youth is renewed like the eagle's.*
PSALM 103:2,5

Restore me, Lord. Give me back the pure desires that were born in my young heart so many years ago. I wanted to help people. I wanted to save the world. I was certain I could run the country. And I longed to become more like You. I was so passionate back then. But growing responsibilities, my progression into adulthood, and motherhood triggered the autopilot mechanism within me. I started just getting by.

I want to fly, Lord. I mean really fly. Toss me up in the air and make my stomach flip with passion and excitement. Let me feel the rush of gratitude that accompanies the fall back into Your arms. "Do it again! One more time, Lord!" I want to climb far above my current vantage point to see the many good things ahead. Have me soar so high that those on the ground look up and see the Master of the sky who commands the wind to lift my wings to new heights.

# A Wise Child

*Better a poor but wise youth than an old but foolish*
*king who no longer knows how to heed a warning.*
ECCLESIASTES 4:13

I get so caught up in what I am supposed to do by society's standards that I miss the gentle leading of Your way. My children redirect me when they express their simple hearts that beat with Your perfect goodness. I am like the foolish king who barrels over and through situations with authority, yet makes decisions without wisdom. I am blinded by my seniority, forgetting that You are Lord over all. I want to honor my children's faith in me by always seeking Your wisdom on their behalf.

Strip me of my royal cloak, the scepter, and the crown. These are false symbols on my being. They are the emblems of a king, but You are the only ruler of this life, Lord. I come before You as a humble adult seeking Your direction. Transform me into a wise child of Your kingdom.

# Covenant of My Youth

*I will remember the covenant I made with*
*you in the days of your youth, and I will*
*establish an everlasting covenant with you.*
EZEKIEL 16:60

I recall days of jumping on a trampoline. I could experiment with twists, flips, and somersaults because the cushioned landing assured me that my body would never hit the hard ground. This is how I feel about the covenant I have with You, Lord. You heard the voice of a scared child long ago, and You answered with Your grace and promises to hold me up for eternity. How it fills me with joy to know that You will have this covenant with my children. They will be able to call out to You with ease. My prayer is that it will be second nature for them to follow Your voice and remain in sweet relationship with You.

I know hard times will be a part of their lives, but I trust You with them for every step—and jump or twist—of the way. I don't doubt for a second that however grand a leap they make, they will land safe in Your hands.

# Purpose

# A Path of Purpose

*Because God wanted to make the unchanging
nature of his purpose very clear to the heirs of what
was promised, he confirmed it with an oath.*
HEBREWS 6:17

I see love as Your purpose, Lord. Is that right? I cannot begin to presume I understand all that You know, but I do understand Your Word. I see how the message of love penetrates all that I read. I try to bring this into my life by showing compassion to others. I try to give it back to You through efforts at service and kindness.

Do I show Your love as I should? Do You call me to a deeper commitment and level of service? I want to be consistent in my representation of You. I long to be an heir of Your promises and Your future. Bring me to a place of understanding and purpose, Lord. I want to wake up each morning grateful and eager to follow Your path of love.

# True Calling

*With this in mind, we constantly pray for you, that our God may make you worthy of his calling, and that by his power he may bring to fruition your every desire for goodness and your every deed prompted by faith.*

2 Thessalonians 1:11

Faith breeds purpose. I have seen this in my life, Lord. When I encounter those who seem so very lost or hopeless, I pray for them. I remember what it was like to have nothing beyond my immediate circumstances. Then You came along and opened my eyes to life beyond life.

You are the fulfiller of dreams. I remind my children of this all the time. I want them to know that You make Your children worthy of a high calling. You meet us where we are and pave the way to eternity. Lord, I thank You for steering us away from hollow endeavors that bear no fruit and no faith, and for leading us with a desire for goodness.

Recess

# Real Laughter

*Sarah said, "God has brought me laughter, and everyone who hears about this will laugh with me." And she added, "Who would have said to Abraham that Sarah would nurse children? Yet I have borne him a son in his old age."*

GENESIS 21:6-7

Miracles do happen, Lord. I am not telling You anything You don't know. But today I reflect on how amazing Your acts of grace and greatness are in my daily life. I look at my children and instantly remember the first moment I held each of them, how the wonder of it all consumed me. I think of Sarah in Scripture and the unimaginable miracle of her motherhood at such an old age. You are such a good God who fulfills His promises.

When faced with the oddities of life and the nobody-will-believe-this moments, I laugh with deep joy. What else can I do? I really think You are playful. You created fellowship with us. Thank You, Lord, for a full relationship—one including laughter, joy, and celebration.

# Dreams Come True

*When the LORD restored the fortunes of Zion,*
*we were like those who dreamed.*
*Our mouths were filled with laughter,*
*our tongues with songs of joy.*
PSALM 126:1-2

I like to ask my children what they have dreamed as soon as they awaken. I find it fascinating how our minds soar to different places and experiences as we slumber. The dreams I have while I am awake relate to happiness, health, and justice. And I take them to You, Lord, in my times of prayer during the day. These precious minutes are my respite from work, routine, and trouble. It takes just a moment in Your presence for me to be filled with great joy.

I want my children to see beyond their nighttime dreams to those You are creating for their journey of life. With gladness, I tell them that You are the maker of my unfolding hopes and dreams and that *they* are one of those dreams! And when I hear them relaying how You have blessed them during the day, that, too, is a dream come true.

# When Today Lacks Joy

*You make known to me the path of life;*
*you will fill me with joy in your presence,*
*with eternal pleasures at your right hand.*
PSALM 16:11

I would not want to repeat the mornings I have had lately, Lord. They've been filled with tears and unexpected arguments with the children. All of a sudden our routine seems to rub them wrong. Forgive me for being so ready to wave good-bye to their little faces so I can turn to You and cry for a while. Your presence not only calms me and releases me from the tension, but You replace my sorrow with joy. True joy. The kind that stays with me during the rest of the day. I'm even able to laugh about my bad mornings. In fact, I can be grateful for the troubles that cause me to run to Your presence for comfort.

God, You still and fill my spirit during this lifetime. I can only imagine how wonderful it will be to reside in Your sweet presence throughout eternity.

# My Soul Worships You

*Sing to him a new song;*
*play skillfully, and shout for joy.*
PSALM 33:3

My instrument may not play a pretty tune, Lord, but I do sing loudly for Your benefit. I let my feet dance, skip, and wander about the house as I shout out my version of a joyful song. I think this is pleasing to You. I hope it is. Somehow this acting out gives me permission to feel Your joy more deeply. I open up my vocal cords and my heart simultaneously, and Your delight flows through me—every bit of me. I'm showing my kids how to do this even though they think I'm nuts. But when they join in and we start singing to You and the praise begins to change our moods and outlooks, there is no denying that Your joy is working in our spirits.

When I become so rigid, so proper, so careful of my steps and my words, help me get over myself, Lord. Because it is through moments of pure happiness that I truly worship You. And it is through times of expressing praise with abandon that my children see the great happiness that comes from loving You.

# Rebellion

# Return of the Rebellious Spirit

*Don't remember the sins of my youth*
*and my rebellious ways;*
*according to your love remember me,*
*for you, LORD, are good.*
PSALM 25:7

I am embarrassed to think of the many sins I have committed over my lifetime. So much weakness. For years I was rebellious, and now and then that same spirit comes over me. Some days I rebel against being a mom. Sometimes I know I'm limiting the attention and encouragement I give to my family out of a place of stubbornness or woe-is-me fatigue.

Look upon this child of Yours with love, Lord. Think of the times when I seek Your will and truly abide by Your Word. I pray those times are becoming more frequent. Forgive me for the sins of my youth and those that creep into my life as a mom and woman of God. Give me strength to follow Your voice through those times of anger or selfish rebellion so that I become a vessel of Your love and grace for my family.

# Getting Back to Your Light

> *"There are those who rebel against the light,*
> *who do not know its ways or stay in its paths."*
> JOB 24:13

On particularly bad days, Lord, I see one of my children wallow in self-pity or resist Your light and the words of Your hope that I share. I know my kid is in a battle without even realizing it or being able to articulate it. In these times, a young mind and heart don't feel worthy of Your love. As You know, I've felt the same way a time or two. I have such empathy for my child because I know what it is like to be scared and unsure. I know what it is to resist the belief that Your love covers me always.

No matter how much we resist Your grace, Lord, don't give up on us. Reach for us. Seek us. Even in our rebellion, the power of our Savior's love seeps into our bones and becomes a part of us. Lord, may we welcome Your light and be willing to walk the path it illuminates this week.

# Working with You

*"Far be it from us to rebel against the LORD
and turn away from him today by building
an altar for burnt offerings, grain offerings
and sacrifices, other than the altar of the LORD
our God that stands before his tabernacle."*

JOSHUA 22:29

God, I work hard to create a great home for my family. You see the effort I make and the desire I have to build a life. Sometimes this passion is so strong I fight You for control of these blessings. How counterproductive! Is it pride? A lack of faith? Tell me, Lord. And help me overcome my areas of rebellion.

I pray I never mold these blessings into ungodly altars. I give this life back to You with a trusting spirit. To be Your faithful servant, I need to do this. Give me strength. Let me begin each day with prayers of thanksgiving and a renewed commitment to make every word and deed and accomplishment an offering to You.

## Strength for the Race

*I have fought the good fight, I have
finished the race, I have kept the faith.*
2 TIMOTHY 4:7

The same strong spirit within me is definitely in my
children. I see myself in their actions and attitudes. I
hear myself repeat my parents' words of warning and correction on a daily basis. Lord, in those moments when
I'm frustrated and pray desperately for patience and
peace, help me to see the positive aspects of this nature.

Remind me of my past trials. Let me see how at
each of my low points, my strong spirit kept me deter-
mined in my faith. I persevered and fought the good
fight. Next time I am in a stand-off with my kids, turn
my despair into celebration. Help me embrace their
strength; I know it will serve them and You well.

# Falling Down

# When I Stumble

*The Lord is my light and my salvation—*
*whom shall I fear?*
*The Lord is the stronghold of my life—*
*of whom shall I be afraid?*

PSALM 27:1

cower at the sight of certain insects. Heights send fear shivers down my spine. And I was afraid of the dark for so long as a child. In these situations, I have relied on Your Word to see me through, Lord. Now when I calm the fears of my children, I share Psalm 27:1. When I face uncertain risk or known troubles, I return to the stronghold of my life—my faith in You.

I pray my children will always seek Your strength in times of worry and anxiety. May my example lead them to Your feet when fear enters their lives. As for me, I will continue to rely on Your light to find my footing when fear causes me to stumble.

# Why Do I Doubt Your Help?

*He went in and said to them, "Why all this commotion and wailing? The child is not dead but asleep." But they laughed at him.*
MARK 5:39-40

I have laughed at You before. In Your face, even. I am not proud of this, Lord. I don't recognize I'm doing this until remorse and regret set in. When I fall to the deepest depths of sorrow or confusion, You promise hope will come. Healing will come. But I resist hearing these words of truth. It's as if I cannot believe one more time, though You have always been faithful. I laugh to protect myself from being hurt.

Why does hardship harden my heart and cause doubt to replace what I know to be true? Lord, please remove this behavior from my ways. When my brokenness refuses to believe Your promises will be fulfilled, my spirit is crying out to You, "Please prove me wrong, Lord."

# Humble Worship

*Who is wise and understanding among you? Let
them show it by their good life, by deeds done
in the humility that comes from wisdom.*
JAMES 3:13

was flat on my face, Lord. You saw me. I was caught
in a very humbling situation. Thank goodness I had
enough wisdom to accept it, to regain an upright position, and to view the humiliation as an opportunity to
let go of pride and reach for Your strength. Thank You
for these times, Lord. Really. If I controlled the world or
at least my slice of it, I would never humble myself. Forgive me for the prideful times when I pretend to have
my act together. Give me wisdom and the good life—
the one that includes humility. If I don't practice humility and honor the chances to fail and stumble, then I
will never be showing my children what it means to
depend solely on You for their worth.

And next time I am flat on my face, may I use the
convenient position to bow down and worship You.

# Slow Motion

*Reach down your hand from on high;*
*deliver me and rescue me*
*from the mighty waters,*
*from the hands of foreigners*
*whose mouths are full of lies,*
*whose right hands are deceitful.*
PSALM 144:7-8

I am slipping, Lord. A little bit each day I drift toward depression and unhappiness. I am believing the world's lies again. I diminish the value of my life and my family each time I nod in submission to deception. I reach up for Your hand. Please rescue me from the confusion of sorrow.

Lord, see me in my time of trouble. I am not strong enough to do this on my own. I am well practiced at falling, but I still struggle with asking for help. So please, Lord, hear my cries. Only You can rescue me.

Why?

# Asking Questions

*My God, my God, why have you forsaken me?*
*Why are you so far from saving me,*
*so far from my cries of anguish?*
*My God, I cry out by day, but you do not answer,*
*by night, but I find no rest.*
PSALM 22:1-2

Lord, why are You distant when I need You here beside me? My situation requires Your attention. I hear nothing. I feel disconnected and alone. For days I have waited for Your acknowledgment. Do You roam the heavens preoccupied with the needs of others? Meet me, here, right now. This moment, Lord.

I am throwing a tantrum. It's similar to the mighty one my child threw this weekend. I wouldn't blame You if You refused to listen to my shout of despair. I question You because I am so desperate. In the stillness of my soul, I know better. I sense the distance is my doing. In my anger, I have closed off my spirit to Your Words of comfort and salvation. My screams of neglect are drowning out Your answer of mercy. My accumulating pile of wants is blocking my view of Your many gifts. Silence my accusations, Lord. When the rush of angst fades and I sit exhausted and sheepish in Your presence, help me lean into Your grace with absolute surrender.

# Still the Storms Within

*He replied, "You of little faith, why are you so
afraid?" Then he got up and rebuked the winds
and the waves, and it was completely calm.*
MATTHEW 8:26

My steps of faith are quite wobbly. As though I have
been out to sea for too long. In a way, this is true.
The pace of my life causes me to lose sight of my rock,
my shore—You. I have nothing to anchor me to truth
and understanding. Discernment flows with the hazardous current, and I am left questioning You and Your
presence.

Heal my unbelief, Lord. Cease the torrential rains
of fear that blind me. I want to see Your face as Your
direction silences the thunder, parts the clouds, and
calms my spirit. You who created all of nature—all of
*me*—are worthy of my trust. Let me walk fearlessly to
Your arms. Like a toddler, I might stumble on the way
to my parent's secure embrace, but I will get there, Lord,
even if I have to crawl.

# Hearing Your Response

*Why do you call me, "Lord, Lord," and
do not do what I say? As for everyone who comes
to me and hears my words and puts them into
practice, I will show you what they are like.*
LUKE 6:46-47

My family has recently experienced a repeated crisis. Actually, it's more drama than true disaster. But as I prayerfully examine our situation, I realize we are in this place again because we have asked for Your help but have then only paid attention to bits of Your guidance. We have applied only a portion of Your wisdom toward a remedy. I become so frustrated when my children ask for help and then reject the advice I give! And here we are doing the same to You as a family.

When I say "Lord, Lord" and relay my list of troubles, I am venting rather than asking for guidance. Clenched fists are never in position to receive. I know this is true! So this time we are going to listen to Your response to our prayers for help. We will heed Your Word, Your instruction, and Your wisdom. We will be a family that calls on You and then listens to Your response.

# Figuring Out Your Mysteries

*Beyond all question, the mystery from which
godliness springs is great: He appeared in the
flesh, was vindicated by the Spirit, was seen by
angels, was preached among the nations, was
believed on in the world, was taken up in glory.*
1 TIMOTHY 3:16

My children ask me "Why?" about every little thing they see and experience. It is their nature to desire understanding. Have I lost my desire to ask You questions? Do I glide on through my life without seeking true understanding? I should be consumed by my desire to understand Your mysteries, Lord. Better yet, maybe someday I will learn to delight in Your mysteries and allow faith to be strengthened in the unknowns.

I don't question You or Your existence, yet I have many unanswered questions about life, death, heaven, and the future my children will have. I come to You now with these inquiries, and I pray You'll receive these questions. I know there will be many that follow. I am Your child; it is my way.

# Boldness

# Calling on Your Name

*When I called, you answered me;*
*you greatly emboldened me.*
PSALM 138:3

Before I had a child, I whispered to You my hope that one day I would be a mom. You answered me by giving me a deep peace and assurance. There were still times after that when I wasn't sure whether it would happen, but the peace never left me. I knew that whatever course my life took, You would shape the desires of my heart to fit the desires You had for me. Now that I am a mom, I'm able to share with my family how to call on You and wait on Your response with absolute certainty that an answer will come. May my family always know the power of Your name and receive the gift of an emboldened spirit when they call on that precious name!

# The Hope of Being Heard

*This is the confidence we have in*
*approaching God: that if we ask anything*
*according to his will, he hears us.*
1 JOHN 5:14

I'm on my knees today, Lord. I come to You with a heavy heart. You know the needs of my family. I ask that Your will be done in our circumstances. My human view is limited, but I know You are moving in our lives this very moment in ways seen and unseen.

I approach You with full confidence because You promise to hear me. Every part of my being trusts this. My heart swells and tears well up when I rise to my feet. With such gentleness, You steady me and set me on the path of faith with renewed boldness. Thank You, Lord, for holding me close when I am weary, and for holding my family up in Your amazing strength.

# Brave Steps

*"Be strong and courageous. Do not be afraid;*
*do not be discouraged, for the L*ORD *your*
*God will be with you wherever you go."*
JOSHUA 1:9

I watched my brave child face a big fear this week. I reluctantly let go of a trembling hand and witnessed my kid's courageous steps toward the unknown. Our prayers together in advance had given both of us confidence to handle the moment. God, in times like this I understand that You are raising me as much as I am raising my child. The growing pains don't stop, but the faith doubles with each stride taken in Your strength.

My family and I are deepening our dependence on You during each new season of life. Wherever we are, Your presence is a constant. You go ahead of us, and You come alongside us. What a comfort it is to know that even when I am not there for each of my children's steps forward, You are.

# When the Children Lead

*When the chief priests and the teachers of the law
saw the wonderful things he did and the children
shouting in the temple courts, "Hosanna to the
Son of David," they were indignant. "Do you hear
what these children are saying?" they asked him.
"Yes," replied Jesus, "have you never
read, 'From the lips of children and infants
you, Lord, have called forth your praise'?"*
<small>MATTHEW 21:15-16</small>

Jesus, You are calling me to pay attention. You are asking me to listen to my kids for Your words of wisdom. You speak so profoundly through the mouths of the youth. Their pure trust isn't hindered by the cynicism or guarded belief that can plague my thoughts. When they turn to You in prayer, they wholly and boldly lift up their day, their dreams, and their hopes for every friend and family member, including the pets. They don't hesitate one moment to proclaim You the keeper and Lord of their lives.

I'm listening closely to them and to You, Jesus, and my spirit is refreshed. Tonight and the nights that follow, this mom's prayers and praises are going to be a lot more childlike.

## About the Author

**Hope Lyda** is an author whose devotionals, novels, and prayer books, including the popular *One-Minute Prayers™ for Women*, have sold over one million copies. Her inspirational books reflect her desire to embrace and deepen faith while journeying to God's mystery and wonder.

Hope has worked in publishing for more than 20 years, writing and coming alongside other writers to help them shape their heart messages. As a trained spiritual director, she loves to help others enter God's presence and pay attention to their authentic, unique life and purpose. Her greatest joy is to find ways to extend these invitations through the written word.

## More prayerful reads from Hope Lyda

*One-Minute Prayers® for Women Gift Edition*

*One-Minute Prayers® for Comfort and Healing*

*One-Minute Prayers® to Begin and End Your Day*

*One-Minute Prayers® from the Bible*

*Life as a Prayer: Devotions to Inspire,*
*Invitations to Be Still (2017 release)*

*Available in e-book only:*

*One Minute with God for Women*

*One-Minute Prayers® for Young Women*

*Hip to Be Square (fiction)*

*Altar Call (fiction)*

*Life, Libby, and the Pursuit of Happiness (fiction)*